For Emma and the colorful Carly Beal
—A. G.

For Mary Blair; and to Sylvia Stack and Gloria Manny,
the two most colorful women I know
—J. T.

For Dad, who lived colorfully
—B. B.

ATHENEUM BOOKS FOR YOUNG READERS
An imprint of Simon & Schuster Children's Publishing Division
1230 Avenue of the Americas, New York, New York 10020
Text copyright © 2017 by Amy Guglielmo and Jacqueline Tourville
Illustrations copyright © 2017 by Brigette Barrager
Photograph of Mary and Lee Blair on p. 45 copyright © 2017 by Getty Images / Hart Preston
All rights reserved, including the right of reproduction in whole or in part in any form.
ATHENEUM BOOKS FOR YOUNG READERS is a registered trademark of Simon & Schuster, Inc.
Atheneum logo is a trademark of Simon & Schuster, Inc.
For information about special discounts for bulk purchases, please contact Simon & Schuster Special
Sales at 1-866-506-1949 or business@simonandschuster.com.
The Simon & Schuster Speakers Bureau can bring authors to your live event. For more information or
to book an event, contact the Simon & Schuster Speakers Bureau at
1-866-248-3049 or visit our website at www.simonspeakers.com.
Book design by Ann Bobco
The text for this book was set in Itchy Handwriting.
The illustrations for this book were rendered digitally.
Manufactured in China
0823 SCP
10 9
Library of Congress Cataloging-in-Publication Data
Tourville, Jacqueline, author.
Pocket full of colors : the magical world of Mary Blair, Disney artist extraordinaire /
Jacqueline Tourville and Amy Guglielmo ; Illustrated by Brigette Barrager.
pages cm
ISBN 978-1-4814-6131-3 (hardcover)
ISBN 978-1-4814-6132-0 (eBook)
1. Blair, Mary, 1911–1978—Juvenile literature. 2. Animators—United States—Biography—Juvenile
literature. 3. Women animators—United States—Biography—Juvenile literature.
I. Guglielmo, Amy, author. II. Barrager, Brigette, illustrator. III. Title.
NC1766.U52B5768 2017
709.2—dc23
[B]   2015022844

POCKET FULL OF
COLORS

The magical world of Mary Blair, Disney artist extraordinaire

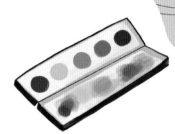

Amy Guglielmo and Jacqueline Tourville

Illustrated by Brigette Barrager

𝒜
atheneum

Atheneum Books for Young Readers

New York London Toronto Sydney New Delhi

Under a wide blue sky,
on a red dirt road,
in a lemon-yellow house,
there lived a little girl named Mary.

Other children collected marbles or dolls,
but Mary collected colors
of every shade and every hue.

One day Mary's parents announced
they were moving out West.

As she waved good-bye to the yellow house,
Mary tucked her friend lemon in her pocket.

Mary would miss the happy home.
But she had new colors to collect.

Driving across the sun-bleached desert,
Mary spied russet, taupe, and sienna.

When she arrived in California, she glimpsed the azure ocean
and found groves of golden fruit dripping from viridian trees.

In the city, she discovered steel-gray buildings and mauve-tinted skies.

Mary opened her sketchbook.
She mixed her paints.
She would save these shades for just the right time.

When she was older, Mary went to art school. She met Lee.
He showed her rosy pink and blushing red.
She kept those colors in her heart.

Together, Mary and Lee painted rainbows.
But it was the Great Depression and people were poor.
No one was buying rainbows. Except one place . . .

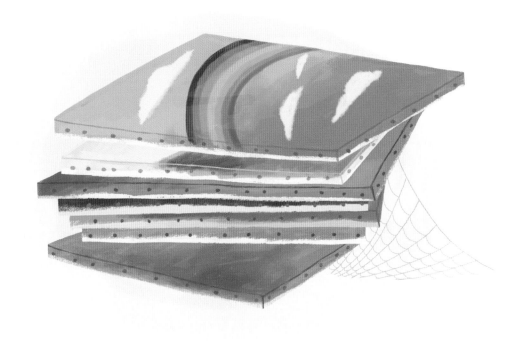

Mary landed a job at Walt Disney Studios,
one of the first women ever to be hired.

Finally, a place for her colors to run
and dance
and play as they pleased!

HOLLYWOODLAND

ANIMATION

DISNEY AVE.

MICKEY ST.

ANIMATION

INBETWEEN

LAYOUT DEPT.

SPECIAL FX

INK & PAINT

But on her first day of work,
the men in charge
didn't want to talk about cerulean
or celadon or cerise.
They were only interested in
black and white.

Mary was told to follow the rules.

She tried, but her colors were too vivid, too wild.
When Mary turned in her work, all her ideas were rejected.

Twinkling emerald skies?
The men turned them blue.

Magenta horses that could fly?
The men made them brown
and put them in a stable.

Peach giraffes with tangerine spots?

Her bosses just shook their heads.
They didn't know what to make
of her art.

But Walt, the man who owned the company, did.

He loved her colors so much, he asked Mary to join him
on a trip to South America to meet some new ones.

Mary delighted in the colors of Brazil, Argentina, and Peru. She worked hard to capture the vibrant scenery. When it was time to go home, Mary's bags burst with fuchsia, teal, aquamarine, indigo, lime green, and banana yellow.

After Mary returned to Disney, her concept art for the studio's upcoming films grew even more adventurous as she drew upon the eye-popping shades she'd observed in South America. *Cinderella* needed a teal pumpkin coach, the caterpillar in *Alice in Wonderland* could only be aquamarine, and the mermaids in *Peter Pan* simply had to be lime green!

This time, some of Mary's ideas were accepted. But most of her art was still considered too modern, too abstract, and just not right.

Mary's colors encouraged her to leave the men with their black lines and strict rules.

So she did.

Mary quickly found new work designing advertisements, illustrating
picture books for children, and creating sets for plays and television
commercials. She enjoyed the freedom of these new jobs.
But Mary missed Walt.

Then one day, out of the blue . . .

her phone rang.

It was Walt!

"Mary, I have a project for you. I need your wild and beautiful colors!" his voice boomed. Walt explained his idea to build a magical ride that would teach people about cultures from around the world. The ride had to be full of color, which meant there was only one person for the job. "Mary, you know about colors I've never even heard of before!"

Mary smiled.

And then she frowned, as she remembered the rules and the lines and the men in charge who didn't understand her colors or her style of art.

There was only one way to answer.

"Yes!" said Mary.
But her yes came with a condition.
This time, Mary wanted to be the one in charge.

Walt welcomed her aboard.

Mary's paints seemed to sparkle
when she hung up the phone.
She had never been to places like
China or Morocco or Kathmandu . . .

but her colors had.

Sitting down to work, she squeezed out dabs of paint.
Lemon yellow, aquamarine and azure, mauve, taupe and tangerine,
russet, sienna and steel gray, celadon, cerulean, cerise, magenta,
teal, indigo, and emerald shined from her palette.
And when she picked up her brush,
the colors Mary had so carefully
collected all her life took
her on a trip around
the globe.

When the work was done and the ride opened,
people gasped in awe.

It's a Small World was a sensation.

When it was Mary's turn to take the ride, she leaned back in the boat and let her colors wash

over her. It was a world of laughter, a world of smiles. And color, color, color everywhere.

This, at last, was Mary's world.

AUTHORS' NOTE

Looking back, we're pretty sure it was during a conversation about It's a Small World when we realized our mutual admiration for the art and designs of Mary Blair. While her whimsically colorful style—found everywhere from classic Disney films to Little Golden Books—is easy to recognize, not many people recognize her name. And even fewer know about Mary Blair's determination to use her visionary talent to the fullest.

When Mary began working for Walt Disney Studios in 1940, her job was to create preliminary sketches to guide the look and feel of the studio's animated films. Her sketches were handed off to the "Nine Old Men," the nickname for Disney's core group of supervising animators who created some of Disney's first major works, including Snow White, and pioneered many of the rules and guiding principles of animation that are still in use today.

Mary drafted sketches for Dumbo, an early version of Lady and the Tramp, and a sequel to Fantasia that was never produced. Her supervisors rejected virtually all of her colorful and modern designs. After one frustrating year on the job, Mary quit.

However, in the brief time she was there, Mary made a true friend at Disney Studios—Walt Disney himself! Walt was so impressed with her colorful style that he invited Mary to join El Grupo, the select group of Disney illustrators who toured and sketched in South America in 1941 as part of a US Goodwill tour.

Mary rejoined Disney Studios as an art director upon her return from the tour. She worked on The Three Caballeros, a film inspired by the animators' trip. This time, Mary's concept sketches—a playful little train chugging its way through a vibrantly shaded jungle—made it onto the big screen.

Heartened by this success, Mary continued on—and although a handful of her breathtaking designs were incorporated into classic films like Cinderella, Alice in Wonderland, and Peter Pan, once again, most of Mary's ideas were considered too abstract, and even too colorful!

When Mary decided to leave Disney Studios again in 1953, she had little trouble finding more work. Moving to New York, Mary became an in-demand commercial artist, Broadway set designer, and picture book illustrator. Her Little Golden Book *I Can Fly* by Ruth Krauss is still in print today!

Mary had become a very busy artist, but when Walt called her up to design that special ride for the 1964 World's Fair, she couldn't refuse his incredible offer. Finally free to create the art she wanted, Mary's palette overflowed. As fellow Disney artist Rolly Crump, an assistant on the It's a Small World project, said, "I don't think she mixed paint very much. She used all and every color. That's the thing I learned from her: 'Don't be afraid of color, Rolly.'"

When Mary Blair died in 1978, it seemed like her art would end up as a footnote in the history of Walt Disney Studios. This began to change as emerging animators rediscovered Disney's Golden Age, and with it, Mary Blair. In 1991, Mary Blair was named a Disney Legend, and in 2011, a Google Doodle was published honoring what would have been Mary's one hundredth birthday.

In 2014 the Walt Disney Family Museum hosted the first retrospective of her work. As room after colorful room burst with Mary's joyful, exuberant art, it became clear what Mary had created during her lifetime: pure magic.

Mary and Lee Blair, sketching in Brazil, 1941